MEAL PREP

A STEP BY STEP GUIDE TO PREPARING HEALTHY WEIGHT LOSS LUNCH RECIPES FOR WORK OR SCHOOL USING EASY MEAL PREP TECHNIQUES TO SAVE TIME AND MONEY

Table of Contents

Introduction

These days most of us lead an action-packed life due to a demanding schedule either at work or looking after our families at home. Time-consuming meal preparation eats up a lot of our time, and yet most of us care about health and want to enjoy eating nutritious and healthy home-cooked food. What could be more satisfying if we prepare it for our family and loved ones?

If you are a food enthusiast and love to cook but have limited time, this cookbook will be a lifesaver for you. As the title suggests, all the meals and dishes can be cooked in less than an hour. Thus, it saves a lot of your time and energy.

Good eating brings joy and happiness in two ways. Firstly, it creates satisfaction in eating delicious food and well-prepared food. The other one is, it provides buoyant health, joy, and vitality that comes from a wise choice of foods. Both are important in having good nutrition.

The method in the way of cooking can be adjusted to whatever ingredients you have in your fridge or what is available in your cupboard. You may also substitute another ingredient in replacement for the one missing or one that you don't have. The utensils and kitchen equipment needed are also the basic ones that we have in our home, which makes for you cooking a lot more easy and convenient.

Feeding our family a well-balanced diet and healthy food is very important. Taking the time to ensure that we provide right food for them is what makes a happy and healthy family. The secret of eating healthy food is not only about planning but also ensuring that you have plenty of healthy recipes that are available for you because sometimes it's quite hard to plan if we do not have something that can serve as our guide. That is why we put altogether some of the quick and easy recipes on this book that will suit everyone's preference especially for Mom's who are always on the go.

Meal Planning

The planning and preparation of meals is very important because next to water that we drink, and the air that we breathe, it is the food that we eat that is essential for our existence. Without food, our body cannot function well, and too much of it will also cause many abnormalities in our body organs. That is why planning plays a very important role in making sure that we prepare nutritious food based on the daily value of nutrients that our body needs to be able to achieve a healthy and well balanced-diet life.

Meal planning, preparing and serving is an art, which develops through thought and inspiration. Planning a variety of food is important. Well-balanced meals keep your family well nourished. It will also build a happy home life.

Food is classified into different main constituent groups such as water, vitamins, minerals, protein, carbohydrates, and fats.   We need to know and understand what are the effects of this food in our body for us to eat properly are.

Menu prepping may bring fun or hard work, but the real importance of it is to avoid a repetitive course of the meal that we provide for our family or even for ourselves. In meal planning, the nutritional value is the most important thing that we need to consider. We eat food not just for fun or pleasure but rather we eat for health purpose.

In meal planning, there are several important points that one needs to consider. They are as follows:

(a) **Nutritional Value** – 6 basic needs of our body are as follows:

    ✓ *Leafy green vegetables & fruits* :

One or more daily (e.g., spinach, cabbage, apple, mango)

✓ *Vitamin C-rich food :*

One or more servings daily (e.g., papaya, strawberries, tomatoes)

✓ *Succulent vegetables & fruits :*

Two or more daily (e.g., cucumber, watermelon, avocado)

✓ *Fat-rich food :*

Three tablespoons daily (e.g., butter, margarine, chocolate, coconut milk)

✓ *Protein-rich food :*

Three servings daily (e.g., gluten, meat, fish, poultry)

✓ *Carbohydrate-rich food :*

Four or more daily serving (e.g., rice, bread, oatmeal, root crops)

(b) **Economy in meals** – Strategies that you may use in purchasing and storing food that will help to save money wisely.

> ➤ Set up a budget intended for the food necessities

> ➤ Make a list of what you need to buy before heading to grocery store or public market

> ➤ Compare prices in different market or grocery stores

> ➤ Try to minimize waste in food and prepare only what you can eat

➢ Buy perishable only when needed

➢ Do not stock up too much food in your fridge and cupboard

➢ Check on the expiry dates of all the items you buy especially canned goods

(c) **Palatability** – This includes the taste and appearance of the food especially if we want our young ones to be able to eat the food that we prepared for them.

(d) **Variety in food** – Variety in meal planning is important to make sure that we do not continuously eat the same kind of food every day or even weekly.

✓ Plan meal according to season

✓ Avoid repeating the same kind of food in one meal

✓ Combine flavors

✓ Use sauces to add flavors

✓ Be aware of the serving temperature of the food

(e) **Safety and Sanitation** – All foods need proper storage to avoid contamination especially if we are going to keep it for a while. Always remember to follow proper temperature guidelines for storing food. An unsanitary method of handling food preparation may cause diseases and even death. Safety measures are very important and very simple to follow. It may even save a lot on Doctor's bills.

(f) **Preferences of family member** – In food preparation, remember to consider the feeling of satisfaction it can give for yourself and your family. The quality of food also depends on the rate of digestion of the person who is going to eat the food.

Benefits of Meal Prepping

One of the best benefits of meal prepping is saving time. Wise use of time in early preparing of meals means having additional time for other chores or activities. Wise planning, with effective time management, can help an individual to become more efficient. Here are some of the benefits that you can get from meal prepping ahead of time:

- It saves time for you since you have already a prepared menu for the whole week

- You are able to plan simple and easy-to-prepare food that suits your budget

- It can help you lose weight easier as you can choose the ingredients and portion size.

- Provide time for you to arrange your kitchen utensils in accordance with your preference so that your time in the kitchen is spent efficiently.

- It can reduce stress as you already have everything planned out in advance.

Equipment Needed For Meal Prepping

We can work and do better in the kitchen if we have the right tools, utensils and kitchen equipment available for whenever it is required. Remember, cooking and eating is part of our daily routine in life, and it is the quality and convenience of that kitchen aid that is truly important especially for the Mother's out there, as they are the ones who usually manage the kitchen. When buying equipment, we need to consider other important aspects not just only the price. Here are some of the most essential and commonly used kitchen utensils:

Aluminum – Most commonly used all round utensils. Less expensive and provide even heat distribution no matter what kind of range you use.

Stainless Steel – A bit expensive but it is easy to clean and keep shiny. Just make sure to cover every time you use it for cooking to evenly spread the heat and keep the pots from getting dark spots.

Glass – Use for baking in the oven

Cast Iron – Use for skillet preparation, make sure to keep seasoned otherwise, it will rust.

Teflon – Helps in preventing the food from sticking to the pot, especially if the food is overheated. Easier to wash and clean. Remember to use a plastic spatula or wooden spoon to prevent scratches. A Teflon non-stick pan also requires less oil to be used.

Here are the lists of kitchen tools that must be present in your kitchen. These are the most commonly used utensils used for food prepping:

Grater	Measuring Cups
Wooden Mixing Spoon	Measuring Spoons
Scissors	Eggbeater
Can Opener	Flour Sifter
Melon Scraper	Bottle Opener
Wooden Chopping Board	Small Paring Knives
Wire Strainer	Chopping Knife
Wire Whip	Bread Knife
Pancake Turner	Butter Knife
Ice Scraper	Soup Ladle
Coconut Grater	Large Pronged Fork
Cake Pans	Metal Spoon
Muffin Pans	Rubber Scraper
Pie Pan	Ice Pick
Saucepan	Loaf Pan
Kettle	Utility Tray
Colander	Mixing Bowls
Dishtowels	Frying Pan
Potholders	Broiler
Dishcloths Or Sponge	Steel Wool

Storing Of Ingredients

Ingredients must be stored properly and to be put it in an airtight container if necessary. Here are some practical tips on how to store ingredients that we cannot finish the whole quantity or amount of it after cooking one specific meal that we normally buy in plastic packaging:

- Make sure the container that we are going to use are clean and dry before we transfer the dry ingredient such as sugar, salt, baking powder, etc.

- Transfer right away any excess ingredient into a container and store it properly.

- Put a clear label on it before you store it.

- Include the expiry date on the label of each container.

- Make sure the covers are airtight.

- Double check if you have covered it properly right after using it.

- Separate all the dry ingredients from the liquid ingredients.

- Always wipe and clean the outside of the container before storing it.

Prepping Of Ingredients

It is highly advisable to prepare the ingredients for the meal you need to cook or prepare ahead of time, like a day before you plan to cook it. If you normally store your dry ingredients inside your cupboard, you may put it in one place so that it will be easier for you to find it when you need it, and saves a lot of your time as well.

Here are some tips that may help you in prepping out before you start to cook:

- Read the recipe and familiarize it. Prepare a sequence as to how and what you need to do first like soaking, chopping, and pre-cooking, etc.

- Prepare the tools and cookware you will need ahead of time.

- Wash and drain the vegetables you need for cooking.

- Ensure the knives are well-sharpened before using.

- Measure exact amount of ingredient to be used.

- Double check if all the ingredients needed are complete and pre-preparation has been done like grating and chopping.

- Have the ingredients lined-up and are ready to add according to the procedure.

Methods of Cooking Ingredients

Cooking methods have two categories: the dry heating and moist heating.

- Dry heating includes: sautéing, searing, baking, roasting, pan-frying, deep-frying, stir-frying and grilling

- Moist heating includes: simmering, boiling, blanching, braising, poaching, stewing and steaming

As time goes by and as cooking procedures evolve, there are a few modifications done to improve the quality and way of cooking. Choosing the right ingredient and developing the right habit will always be the basic rule in achieving a great result.

- To thicken the sauce, you may use butter, cream or puree.

- Instead of using soy sauce, you can replace it with tamari, which is made from pure soy only.

- Try replacing milk as the main ingredient in making sauces to unsweetened coconut cream.

- You may also use shirataki noodles instead of regular or conventional pasta.

- Browning the meat before adding another ingredient will produce a caramelized crust and adds flavor to the food

- Leafy and green vegetables must be added only just in time to cook the dish. This will keep the bright color, and it won't dominate the taste the rest of the dish.

- It is always best to make a homemade stock either fresh or frozen. If not available, use stock cube instead.

Cooking Tips and Procedures

- Plan Meals Ahead

- Prepare everything a night before the actual cooking of food. Measure the ingredients and put it in a container. You may also do the preparation early morning to have ample time.

- Use the Correct Size of Cookware-Enables proper cooking of food and prevent overflowing of food.

- Avoid Overfilling-Let you cook right amount and quantity of food.

- Keeping the Lid Closed-Prevents slow cooking which will let the heat escape if there is an opening while cooking. Stir food once if needed only.

- Keeping Exact Temperature-Ensure proper usage to prevent a food-safety hazard. The standard temperature must be followed.

- Maximize Flavor and Taste-Richer flavor in cooking can be maximized through slow cooking. This procedure needs time to be able to achieve best results.

- Use the Best Quality Pot-The best result in cooking can be achieved by using the right quality of equipment. Quality always speaks as the most important factor.

Prep, Sauces, Dips, and Dressings

Condiments such as Sauces, Dips, and Dressings add up flavors and taste to the food that we can prepare and serve. Here are some low-carb condiments that we can use and include in our daily diet:

- Mustard – Best for a salad even for burgers and sandwiches. Use Dijon Mustard or flavored mustard except those with honey or sugar ingredient.

- No-sugar-added jams – Create a quick sauce by melting in the microwave oven.

- Vinegar – Red wine has a lot of use and is very versatile for cooking. Cider vinegar is mild while balsamic is sweet.

- Chopped garlic or ginger – Fresh varieties are better, but it is also available in the shake up a bottle. It adds flavor and texture to the food.

- Puree – Basil pesto, garlic puree, tomato puree and olive puree.   Anchovy paste is also another variation.

- Sauces & Syrups – The most commonly used are barbecue sauces and ketchup. Maple syrup also adds sweetness and flavor. Make sure to use the sugar-free and low-carb products.

- Herbs – They heighten the flavor of the food and releases oils. Fresh herb creates a cleaner and purer flavorful taste.

Put It All Together

Fresh produce foods add valuable nutrients to a specific meal as well as texture, color, and appetizing flavors.

- Vegetables – Source of vitamins, fiber, and minerals. Vegetables are packed with carotenoids such as vitamin A, C, E and protects against cancer and heart diseases

- Meat & poultry – Provide protein, iron, zinc, minerals & Vitamin B needed to release energy into our body

- Fish & Seafood – Provide essential minerals and protein. A good source of Omega-3 fatty acids protects against heart diseases, and it also feeds our brain.

- Fresh herbs – Provide delightful fragrance, color, and taste to our meals

A few of our cupboard foods provide essential benefits in creating a great and perfect meal.

- Grains – Includes rice, oats, quinoa, barley, and wheat, which contains nutrients.

- Pulses – Packed with nutrients as well and provide strongly flavored ingredients

- Pasta – Source of carbohydrate, but do not eat too much of it.

- Seeds and nuts – Provide texture and can give body to the cooking.

- Sauces & pastes – Give an outstanding and exciting flavor on the food.

- Spices & dried herbs – Brings out the full flavor. Varieties are better when it is fresh.

Box It All Up

Storing food is necessary because proper storage of food restores quality and maintains the freshness of the food. Here are some of the most commonly used food storage aides that provide and maintain a highly organized kitchen.

- ✓ Canister Set – storage for dry ingredients

- ✓ Bread Box – bread storage

- ✓ Cake Safe – cake storage

- ✓ Cookie Jar – for cookies, small bite-sized pastries, and sweets

- ✓ Set of refrigerator dish with cover – use for leftover food

- ✓ Plastic refrigerator bag – may use for storing vegetables

- ✓ Wax paper – food wrap

- ✓ Aluminum Foil – food cover and food wrap

- ✓ Airtight container – for dry ingredients

- ✓ Sealable bag – used for thawing

Food Storage

Proper storage of food should be an important practice for every household. Food has different classification thus requires proper storage to avoid contamination. Temperature is also an important consideration. It is essential because it determines the freshness of the food. Food is classified into three different categories: perishable, semi-perishable and non-perishable.

Perishable food is a type of food that spoils easily and requires standard temperature storage. Food that keeps best at a low temperature, usually above its freezing point is perishable food. Semi-perishable food, on the other hand, is food that we can keep for a limited time only. While non-perishable food is what we can keep for a longer period like a few weeks or even a few months.

Through proper storage method practice, no food and money will be wasted. Here are some few suggestions on best practices for storing food:

- *Berries* – Must be wrapped in paper and kept cool in a refrigerator. If you put it in a plastic container or glass container make sure to cover it tightly.

- *Bread* – Remember to store it at a room temperature. You may also keep it inside the refrigerator to prevent molds from forming quickly.

- *Cookies* – Crisp cookies must be stored in a can with a loose cover. The soft one needs to be stored in an airtight container.

- *Custard puddings* – These are highly perishable, it needs to be immediately stored in the refrigerator for not more than 24 hours.

- *Pies* – Covered it with aluminum foil or wax paper. You may store it at a room temperature.

- *Potatoes, carrots & onions* – Always keep it in the cool, dry and well-ventilated room.

- *Leafy vegetables* – It should be kept in the refrigerator.

- *Milk, cream & eggs* – Should be kept in the refrigerator always.

- *Shortenings* – Keep closely covered inside the refrigerator.

- *Cheese* – Wrap in waxed paper. Keep in a covered container and grate leftover cheese.

- *Sugars* – Keep it tightly covered in a dry place.

- *Tea & Coffee* – Keep in a cool, dry place.

- *Flour, Cereals & Cake Mixes* – store in a dry place in an airtight container. Can put in the fridge for long keeping.

- *Staple supplies* – Keep in a dry place and cover it tightly.

- *Nuts & coconut* – Put in the refrigerator and cover it tightly.

- *Salad dressing* – Keep at a room temperature or inside the refrigerator. Cover it tightly.

- *Condiments* – Keep it tightly covered. Put in the fridge or kitchen cupboard.

- *Cut lemon, orange & melon* – Store inside the fridge and place cut-side-down on a small plate or in a covered container.

- *Cut onion & garlic* – Place cut-side-down in a cardboard or carton and place inside the fridge and cover it.

How to Store Meat

There are different ways of storing meat depending on the type of it. Here are simple guidelines for proper storing of meat:

- Frozen Meat – Keep in freezer unit and do not unwrap. Keep it frozen all the time until ready to use.

- Fresh Meat – Remove the wrap or plastic and cover it with wax paper. Remember to cover it loosely, leaving both ends open and put it in the refrigerator.

- Ground Meat – Unwrap it and cover loosely using wax paper. Store it same as fresh meat and remember to cook within 24 hours.

- Cooked Meat – Put in a dish and cover tightly with foil. Put it in the refrigerator.

- Smoked Meat – Stored it the same procedure as fresh meat.

- Poultry – Keeps better if whole rather than in pieces. Put in the refrigerator and wrap loosely using wax paper.

- Fresh Fish – Keep in the refrigerator and place it in a tightly covered dish. Cook within 24 hours only.

Thawing & Reheating

Thawing and reheating of food is a process that needs careful attention as it may lead to food poisoning or food contamination. Standard temperatures must be followed to avoid food-borne illnesses.

Proper Thawing of Food:

- DO NOT defrost perishable foods outdoors.

- Refrigerate (poultry, meat, seafood/fish) within 24 to 48 hours or until it is completely thawed.

- If you are in a hurry, you may place the item in a sealable bag and place it in cold water. Take note to change the water every 30 minutes.

- Using a microwave oven: Make sure to remove wrapping and heat it for 6 to 8 minutes using low heat only. Once completely thawed, reheat it using high heat this time.

Proper Reheating Procedure:

- Reheat food at least 165F within 2 hours' time.

- Use a food thermometer to check if the desired temperature has met.

Reheating Leftover Food :

- Heat the food using high heat until steaming hot.

- Stir gradually to encourage even heating

- Make sure to finish food after reheating it

Cooking Tips

- It is always best to use ingredients based on what the recipe provides but if you have a substitute then that is also fine.

- To make half a recipe; you need to reduce the amount of all the listed ingredients into half.

- If the recipe needs less amount of one egg, just beat up one whole egg and take one tbsp of it. You may use excess amount to cook a scrambled egg.

- If you want to increase the amount of the recipe just use twice all the listed ingredient.

- If happen to increase the amount of the ingredients in baking, do take note to use two baking pans. Baking time and temperature always remain the same and do not increase it.

- To make sure that nuts will taste fresh, toast it. Heat it in the microwave oven over moderate heat.

- In making a salad, lemons are used in replacement of vinegar.

- Use herb vinegar that gives an interesting flavor to your salad.

- Pre-soak pasta before you cook it. You will just need around 60 seconds of cooking after soaking it.

- Grate a frozen butter in the mixture for fast and even distribution.

- Caramelized onion faster by adding baking soda to it.

- Grate ginger instead of mincing it.

- To be able to extract more juice, you need to microwave the lemon or lime first.

- Freeze meat for easy slicing.

- Practice the rule of thumb to check the readiness of the steak.

- Add a little bit of lemon to your pan to prevent butter from over-browning.

- Always taste the food before adding any seasoning or condiments.

- Used slice garlic instead of minced garlic to prevent from getting it burned easily.

- Make breadcrumbs out of stale bread instead of throwing it away.

- Honey will never be spoil. It is a type of natural preservative.

- If you put the butter in the freezer, it can last for up to six months.

- To soften butter faster, slice it and put it at a room temperature.

- Always exactly measure the ingredients for baking to avoid erroneous effects.

- Overcooked vegetables lose their nutrients.

- Mushrooms should always be kept dried because they absorb water easily.

- Store fresh herbs in a glass of water inside your refrigerator.

- Practice reading and re-reading your recipe before you start doing it.

- Do not add dressing to your salad until it is time to eat.

- Keep spices away from the source of heat, Spices and herb losses it flavors if exposed to direct heat.

- Homemade meals are good for the heart and soul.

Budgeting and More Tips

A typical family's budget will normally have a big amount of money set for the food. Although it is important, money isn't everything about planning tasty, nutritious meals. A well-balanced meal can also be prepared on a small budget. The most important thing is having the right and correct knowledge as to what, how and when to buy. Less money spent on food means additional money for other needs.

Here are some practical tips on how we can stretch our money out and prevent from going overboard on our set budget for the week:

- Compare prices from another supermarket for you to know who offers lower prices and do your grocery there instead to save money.

- Buy perishable food only if you need it or part of your menu planning for the week.

- Avoid buying expensive goods especially expensive brands. Find an alternative that is much cheaper but always check on the quality of the items that you are buying.

- Buy foods in season especially for fruits as it is cheaper compared to those that are not in season.

- Always make a habit to check your supplies on hand to avoid buying duplicate ingredients and make it a basis of your list before heading to the supermarket.

- Buy quality food for your family to avoid wasting money.

- Buy staple foods in bulk because it is cheaper that way and store them properly.

- Do your groceries during less busy periods to avoid too many crowds and long queues in the supermarkets. It saves a lot of your time.

- Buy food that is enough for your family's consumption.

- Cook enough amount of food for your meals and make sure to finish it to avoid waste of food and money.

- Use leftover food as an additional ingredient for a new meal (e.g., roasted chicken, beef or pork)

- Plant vegetables and herbs in your garden if you have the spare area, that way you ensure a fresh supply of it.

- If you know how to bake, you may bake bread and cookies for your family.

- You may use tofu instead of meat for your ingredient. Meat is more expensive compared to tofu which is cheaper and more nutritious.

- Check the label and expiry of goods you are buying in the grocery especially bottled and canned goods to avoid wasting money.

- Use evaporated milk instead of fresh milk, which is more expensive.

- In buying vegetables, do take note to check the color and always remember to buy only what you will go to use right away as it is not advisable to keep vegetable for long as they are highly perishable items.

- Plan meals one at a time for several days.

- You can switch to buy brown egg if they cost cheaper compared to a white egg. The nutrition value is just the same.

- Use margarine instead of butter. It is a healthy alternative and cheaper compared to butter.

- Stick to your budget and do not go overboard.

- Do not serve too many kinds of dishes at one meal. Rice, one vegetable, and one protein dish are enough.

- Buy only groceries that is intended for a week consumption, that way you make sure you have fresh products available either in your fridge or storage cabinet.

- Buy dry product first before you proceed to fresh section if you are inside the supermarket and doing your grocery. This will keep fresh produce products quality.

- Bring packed meals at work or to school to avoid buying food outside. This is a great way to save money as well.

- Follow the recipes in this book and take the meals to school or work instead of going out to buy food at lunchtime. This is a great way to save money and will be a lot healthier!

How to Follow These Recipes

The following recipes have been devised to give you some ideas for creating healthier lunches in advance that are quick and easy to prepare.

All of the recipes are designed to produce 1 portion for you. I advise you to look at the recipes, find the ones that you like the sound of and then give them a try. You can then prepare these in advance and multiply the ingredients so that you have enough lunches ready throughout the week and leave them in the fridge. Most workplaces have fridges and microwaves these days so you should be able to keep your food refrigerated and warm up when you are ready to eat.

This will save a lot of time, money, and be extremely more beneficial for you if you are someone who goes out and buys lunch every day when you are at work.

Bread, Roll,

Wrap &

Sandwich

Recipes

Bagel Topped with Salmon

Ingredients:

60 gm cooked salmon fillet

1 pc bagels split in half

50 gm reduced-fat soft cheese

1 tbsp chives

Handful of Watercress

¼ cup lemon zest juice

How to make:

Put the flaked salmon in a bowl. Add cheese, chives, ground pepper, lemon zest, and juice. Mix everything and keep chilled until lunchtime.

Lightly toast the bagel halves. Spread the salmon mixture and top each one with a handful of watercress.

Arrange it inside the packed lunch box.

Teriyaki Chicken Burger

Ingredients:

¼ lb. ground chicken

1 tbsp low-carb teriyaki sauce

1 spring onion, chopped

1/2 clove garlic, chopped

1 tsp ginger, peeled & grated

1 tbsp rapeseed oil

1 tsp dark sesame oil

¼ tsp ground black pepper

1-2 lettuce leaves

Mayonnaise dressing

1 slice of cheese

How to make:

Make a patty by combining chicken, spring onions, garlic, teriyaki sauce, ginger, sesame oil and pepper in a medium bowl then shape into a 2 cm thick patty.

Heat the oil over a medium flame. Fry patties until browned for about 5 minutes per side. Serve with hamburger buns and top it with lettuce leaves, slice cheese, and mayonnaise dressing.

Pack the burger in your lunch box and pair it with fresh fruits on the side.

Chickpea Pita with Yogurt Dressing

Ingredients:

1 large whole meal-pita piece of bread

60 gm chickpeas, cooked & drained

1 tbsp 0% fat Greek yogurt

¼ cup beetroot, cooked & grated

1 small carrot, grated

½ tsp harissa paste

Few mint leaves

How to make:

Slice the pita bread in half. Mix beetroot, chickpeas, carrot, and mint, then season. Spread on pita bread the yogurt with harissa mixture then follow with the beetroot mixture and wrapped up inside the lunch box.

Steak Sandwich

Ingredients:

60 grams leftover ground beef

2 pcs whole-meal bread

50 grams mozzarella cheese

2 tbsp scallions, chopped

Hot-pepper sauce

Red pepper flakes

How to make:

Cut the whole-meal bread in half to form a pocket. Fill the bread with shredded mozzarella cheese and leftover ground beef. Microwave it for about 1 minute, or until warm. Season it on top with hot-pepper sauce, red-pepper flakes, or chopped scallions to taste. Arrange the sandwich inside your packed lunch.

Pork Sandwich with Pesto

Ingredients:

60 grams leftover pork

3 tbsp mozzarella cheese

2 slices sourdough bread

3 tbsp of pesto

Handful of Basil leaves

How to make:

Spread pesto on two slices of sourdough bread and a handful of fresh basil leaves on top of it. Put the leftover pork and add a shower of mozzarella cheese. Microwave until cheese melts. Wrap it up inside your lunch box and pair it with fruits on the side.

Grilled Salmon Sandwich

Ingredients:

60 grams leftover grilled salmon

2 tbsp reduced-fat mayonnaise

2 sliced whole-wheat roll

Chili powder

2 slices tomato

Handful of lettuce

1 tsp lime juice

½ tsp garlic, minced

How to make:

Combine reduced-fat mayonnaise, chili powder, lime juice and minced garlic. Stir well to mix. You can add more lime juice to taste if needed. Transfer half of the mayonnaise mixture into a separate container, then refrigerate.

Spread the remaining mayonnaise mixture on the whole-wheat bread. Top it with leftover grilled salmon, lettuce, and a tomato slice. Serve with fruits on the side and packed it inside your lunch box.

Prawn Cocktail Sandwich

Ingredients:

60 gm prawns, cooked & peeled

2 slices wholemeal bread

1 tbsp reduced-sugar ketchup

1 tbsp light mayonnaise

1 tbsp chopped dill

10 gm rocket leaves

¼ cup cucumber, diced

¼ cup cherry tomatoes, halved

½ lemon, cut into wedges

How to make:

Prepare a dressing in a separate bowl, mix the juice from the lemon, mayonnaise, ketchup, half the dill and some seasoning. Add the prawns, tomatoes & cucumber.

Top the bread with rocket leaves and pile on the prawn filling. Scatter the remaining dill, serve with lemon wedges on the side of your lunch box, and wrap it up.

Chicken with Avocado & Carrot Roll

Ingredients:

60 grams chicken breast, shredded

2 pcs tortillas

30 gm low-fat soft cheese

¼-cup rocket leaves

Half of an avocado, sliced

How to make:

Put the cheese over the tortillas and add the chicken, avocado, carrot, and rocket leaves.

Roll up each tortilla and tightly wrap it using cling wrap, twist the ends firmly to seal.

Bean & Chicken Rolls

Ingredients:

60 grams leftover chicken, shredded

1 large tortilla wraps

1 slice pickled jalapeno peppers

2 tbsp kidney beans, drained

1 tbsp spicy salsa

¼-cup spinach leaves

2 cherry tomatoes, halved

How to make:

Heat the tortilla in a microwave oven for about 10 seconds. Put the beans and chicken in the middle, then season over with salsa and scatter with peppers or Tabasco. Put the tomatoes and leaves on top. Bring the bottom of the tortilla up over the filling and fold the sides. Roll it into a tight wrap. Pack up together to keep it tightly inside your packed lunch.

Chicken Wrap

Ingredients:

60 gm leftover rotisserie chicken

¼ cup leftover vegetables, roasted

¼ cup mixed bell peppers (green, orange & red)

1 clove of garlic, minced

1 tbsp reduced-fat mayonnaise

1 whole-wheat tortilla

2 tsp balsamic vinegar

1 tbsp mozzarella cheese, shredded

How to make:

Chop the peppers into a ½ inch, then set aside ½ cup and transfer the remaining 3 ½ cups to a separate container and refrigerate it.

Mix the following ingredients: vinegar, garlic & mayonnaise. Brush the tortilla with the mixture and sprinkle the cheese in the middle, followed by chicken, and all the vegetables. Fold about ½ inch of the tortilla up and then roll it from the side, to make a tight wrap. Pair it with some fruits, pack and go.

Salad

Recipes

Beef with Scallion Salad

Ingredients:

1 cup chopped romaine lettuce

30 gm leftover Asian Beef

1 tbsp blue cheese crumbles

1 small tomato, chopped

1 tbsp scallions, chopped

1 small clove garlic, minced

Extra-virgin olive oil

How to make:

Combine lettuce, tomato, beef, scallions, and garlic. Drizzle with oil and toss well to coat. Top it with the cheese and packed it inside your lunch box.

Tomato Salad with Balsamic Vinegar

Ingredients:

2 pcs large tomato, sliced

Drizzle extra-virgin olive oil

Sea salt to season

1 tbsp balsamic vinegar

Handful basil leaves

How to make:

Slice the tomato and season with a small pinch of sea salt and some ground black pepper. Drizzle over oil and vinegar and scatter over the basil. Arrange it in a lunch box and take it to work.

Tuna with Quinoa Salad

Ingredients:

60 gm albacore tuna in olive oil, drained & flaked

½ red pepper, sliced

1 tbsp olive oil

1 small onion, sliced

1-cup ready-to-eat quinoa

½ red chili, chopped

A few cherry tomatoes, halved

Handful pitted black olives, chopped

How to make:

Fry the pepper & onion in the oil, add the chili and let it cool. Mix the tuna, quinoa, cherry tomatoes, olives & onion mixture together.

Pour over the excess oil from the tuna, season and arrange it in a packed lunch.

Vegetable Salad with Balsamic Vinegar

Ingredients:

¼ cup green bell pepper, chopped

1-cup arugula

1 tbsp extra-virgin olive oil

1 tbsp balsamic vinegar

1 celery, chopped

½ small onion, chopped

How to make:

Whisk the oil and vinegar in a mixing bowl. Add the celery, onion, & pepper. Toss and scatter the arugula on a plate. Top the salad over the arugula. You may add sliced boiled egg and bacon strips on the side of your packed lunch.

Spinach Salad with Bacon Strips

Ingredients:

1 slice bacon strips

½ tsp Canola oil

¼ cup leftover scallops

1 handful spinach

How to make:

Fry 2 slices bacon until crisp. Drain excess oil on paper towels. Combine 2 big handfuls spinach in a salad bowl and crumble on the bacon and drizzle with a little canola oil. Toss and top with the leftover scallops.

Cucumber Salad with cheese and pecans

Ingredients:

2 large lettuce leaves, chopped

1 plum tomato, cut into wedges

1 med cucumber, peeled & cut into cubes

10 gm coarsely chopped mint leaves

10 gm coarsely chopped basil

Olive oil cooking spray

Ground black pepper

Salt

White cheese

Chopped pecans

How to make:

Arrange and combine in a salad bowl: lettuce, tomatoes, cucumber, mint, and basil.

Toss salad with dressing, and put a dash of salt and pepper to taste. Top the salad with cheese and pecans.

Bean-Rice Salad

Ingredients:

60 gm can mixed bean salad, drained

Small bunch coriander, chopped

½ red pepper, chopped

1-cup basmati and wild rice mix

1 spring onion, chopped

¼ cucumber, chopped

Juice 1 lime, plus wedges to serve

2 tsp Cajun spice mix

Grapes

How to make:

Cook the rice according to packaging instructions. Drain and set aside. Stir in cucumber, onion, pepper & beans.

Mix Cajun spice mix with lime juice and some ground black pepper. Pour it over the rice mix, stir using coriander and pack with extra lime wedges. Serve in a lunch box.

Celery & Green Bean Salad

Ingredients:

½ cup green bean, halves

Salt and pepper

¼-cup celery

1-cup boiling water

1 tbsp sweet pickles, chopped

¼ cup mayonnaise

1 tbsp lemon juice

1 tbsp radish

2 small tomatoes

How to make:

Bring green beans to the boil for 7 min. Combine all remaining ingredients and toss gently to coat the mayonnaise evenly. Packed the salad in a lunch box and pair it with fresh fruits.

Potato-Pimiento Salad

Ingredients:

2 tbsp French dressing

2 pcs medium sized potato, cooked

1 tsp salt

1 tbsp onion, chopped

1 tbsp pimiento

½-cup mayonnaise

¼ cup diced celery

How to make:

In a mixing bowl, combine diced potatoes and sprinkle it with salt. Add the remaining ingredients and mix well. Dash a pinch of salt, and pepper to taste. Arrange and packed it in a lunch box. Add some ham on the side.

Cauliflower Salad with Grated Cheese

Ingredients:

2 pcs lettuce leaves

¼-cup cauliflower florets

¼ cup French dressing

1 tsp salt

¼ cup grated cheese

How to make:

Let the cauliflower soak in cold salted water. Rinse and set aside. Cook the cauliflower in boiling water for about 6 min. Drain and let it cool before pouring the French dressing on top. Let it sit in the refrigerator for about half an hour and then add cheese, toss thoroughly and then serve it on top of crisp lettuce. Pack it inside the lunch box with fresh fruits.

Pasta Salad

Recipes

Chicken Pasta Salad with Pesto

Ingredients:

40 gm chicken breast, cooked

70 gm pasta

1 tbsp basil pesto

¼ cup red bell pepper, chopped

¼-cup cherry tomatoes halved

1 tbsp low-fat Crème-Fraiche

How to make:

Cook pasta according to packaging direction, then drain and set aside. Mix red pepper with the cherry tomatoes and chicken in a separate bowl.

Combine the pesto and Crème- Fraiche in a small bowl and toss it onto the pasta, adding the vegetable and chicken. Pack into a container for lunch.

Pasta Salad with Prawn

Ingredients:

70 gm pasta

30 gm prawns, cooked & peeled

20 grams chicken, diced and cooked

1 small carrot, diced

1 spring onion, sliced

1 tsp soft brown sugar

1 tbsp mixed coriander and mint leaves, chopped

1 tsp soy sauce

¼ tsp Thai fish sauce

Zest and juice of 1 lime

How to make:

Cook pasta according to the pack instructions. Drain and set it aside. Mix the pasta with prawns, chicken, carrots, spring onions, coriander, and mint.

Whisk the remaining ingredients together in a separate bowl. Pour over the salad and toss well to coat. Store it in an airtight container until ready to eat.

Tuna Pasta Salad with Balsamic Dressing

Ingredients:

70 gm orecchiette pasta

1 tbsp balsamic vinegar

30 gm tuna in spring water, drained and flaked

20 gm cherry tomatoes, halved

1 tbsp capers, drained

1 small celery, sliced

1 tbsp extra-virgin olive oil

50 gm rocket leaves

Handful basil leaves, to garnish

How to make:

Cook pasta according to packet instructions, drain and rinse in cold water and transfer it to a large bowl.

Add the remaining ingredients to the pasta, season well, and toss to combine. Scatter with the basil on top and place in an airtight lunch box.

Walnuts & Dolcelatte Pasta Salad

Ingredients:

70 gm farfalle

20 gm dolcelatte cheese, diced

1 tbsp balsamic vinegar

1 tbsp walnut oil

1 tsp safflower oil

50 gm mixed salad leaves

20 gm walnuts, chopped

Salt and pepper

How to make:

Bring to boil lightly salted water then add the pasta, let it boil for 8-10 min or cook until tender and firm to the bite. Drain and set aside.

Mix the oil with vinegar. Whisk it well and season to taste with salt and pepper.

Arrange the salad leaves in a lunch box container and add the pasta. Top it with dolcelatte cheese and walnuts. Pour the dressings and toss it lightly, then packed the container and bring for lunch.

Penne Pasta Salad with Broccoli and Tuna

Ingredients:

70 gm dried penne

30 gm broccoli

30 gm cooked tuna

¼-cup garlic mayonnaise

1 tbsp lemon juice

1 small head of celery, sliced

Salt and pepper

How to make:

Wash and drain the lettuce leaves and set it aside. Put it in the refrigerator for 1 hour, or until crisp.

Bring the lightly salted water to the boil, then add the pasta, bring it back to boil again and cook for another 8-10 minutes. Drain the pasta and set aside.

Place the broccoli florets in a bowl and sprinkle with the lemon juice to coat them thoroughly to prevent discoloration. Mix the cooled pasta, apples, walnut halves and celery. Toss the mixture in the garlic mayonnaise. Put a dash of salt and pepper to taste.

Arrange the lettuce leaves into a packed container.

Pasta Salad with Avocado and Olives

Ingredients:

70 gm pasta

¼ cup avocado, diced

2 pcs sun-dried tomato in oil, chopped

2 tbsp olives

1 tbsp grated parmesan cheese

1 spring onion, chopped

50gm rocket, shredded

Salt and pepper

How to make:

Boil the lightly salted water. Add the pasta, and boil it again for 8-10 minutes, or until tender but still firm. Drain and put it in a salad bowl. Add the dressing and toss it well.

Add the spring onions, rocket, avocado, sun-dried tomatoes, olives, and season to taste with salt and pepper and toss again. Sprinkle the salad with the parmesan cheese and pack it in a container for lunch.

Green Beans and Corn Pasta Salad

Ingredients:

20gm green beans

70 gm pasta

20 gm corn kernels

1 tbsp olive oil

1 small onion, chopped

1 garlic clove, chopped

1 small carrot, thinly sliced

1 tsp red wine

2 tsp red wine vinegar

Parmesan cheese

Salt

How to make:

Cook the pasta according to packet instructions. Drain and set aside for a while.

Heat the oil in a pan. Add the onion and add garlic, green beans, carrots, corn kernels, and cook for 2-3 min. Add the wine, pasta, and vinegar and let it boil under medium fire. Mix everything and sprinkle with parmesan cheese.

Cucumber Lime Pasta Salad

Ingredients:

70 gm pasta

1 tbsp lime juice

1 tbsp olive oil

1 tsp Thai fish sauce

1 spring onion, sliced

1 tsp clear honey

½ cucumber, cut into chunks

1 tsp fresh mint, chopped

1 tomato cut into wedge

Salt and pepper

How to make:

Cook pasta according to packet instructions. Drain and toss the pasta in the oil.

Mix honey, fish sauce, lime juice in a separate saucepan, and add cucumber, onion, tomato, and mint, then add steak and mix well. Put a dash of pepper and salt to taste. Put the pasta in a container and top it with the sauce mixture, toss and pack it in a lunch box.

Prawn with Melon Pasta Salad

Ingredients:

40 gm cooked prawns

70 gm dried green Fusilli

2 tbsp extra-virgin olive oil

¼-cup melon balls

2 tsp red wine vinegar

½ tsp Dijon mustard

2 tsp flat-leaf parsley, chopped

2 tsp basil, chopped

1 stagioni lettuce

Salt and pepper

How to make:

Cook pasta as per packet instructions. Drain and set aside and toss in 1 tbsp of oil.

Peel the prawns, put it in a bowl, and set aside. Scoop out balls from the melon using a melon baller and add it to the prawns.

Whisk together the red wine vinegar, oil, parsley and basil in a small bowl and season it to taste. Add the pasta to the prawns and melon balls, toss and pour the mixture.

Arrange the lettuce in the lunch box and add the pasta to the mixture.

Chicken Medley Pasta Salad

Ingredients:

40 gm boneless chicken, cut into strips, cooked

70 grams pasta

15 gm white beans

1 tbsp mayonnaise

1 tsp pesto

2 tsp sour cream

15 gm black pitted olives

Salt and pepper

How to make:

Cook pasta evenly according to package direction.

Drain it and set it aside.

In a separate bowl, mix the mayonnaise, sour cream and pesto and put a dash of seasoning to taste. Add the remaining ingredients together with the pasta and mayonnaise mixture and toss it. Transfer it to a container.

Vegetable

Recipes

Vegetarian Fried Rice with Egg

Ingredients:

1 fresh red chili, chopped

30 gm corn kernels

1 tbsp vegetable oil

1 garlic clove, chopped

30 gm mange tout, halved

1 tbsp soy sauce

2 tsp brown sugar

1 egg, beaten

1 small onion, sliced

1 cup rice, cooked

Crispy onion for topping (optional)

How to make:

Heat the oil and fry the garlic and chilies for 2-3 minutes. Add the corn kernels, and mange tout and stir-fry for 2-3 minutes before adding the soy sauce, and sugar. Stir in the rice.

Put the mixture to one side of the wok. Add the eggs to the wok and stir until lightly set before combining with the rice mixture.

Potato Casserole with Lemon

Ingredients:

1 cup potatoes, sliced

1 small red onion, cut into wedges

1 tbsp olive oil

½ tsp ground coriander

½ tsp ground cumin

1 small garlic clove, crushed

¼ cup zucchini, sliced

Pinch of cayenne pepper

¼ carrot, sliced

1 lemon, grated

2 tsp chopped fresh coriander

Salt and pepper

50 ml vegetable stock

How to make:

Clean the potatoes slice and set aside. In a mixing bowl, combine all the ingredients and mix well. Heat oil in a saucepan and cook the mixture for 5 minutes. Now, place potatoes in a casserole dish and then pour the mixture over the potatoes. Bake until the potatoes turn golden. Transfer in a lunchbox. Enjoy!

Buttered Potato with Parsley

Ingredients:

1 tsp chicken seasoning

½-cup water

1 cup sliced potatoes

1 tsp parsley flakes

2 tbsp melted butter

How to make:

Clean the potatoes and peel them. Boil water with the potatoes and seasoned stock base. Reduce the heat after boiling and cook until tender for 25 min and drain. Melt the butter and add seasoning, and pour over the potatoes.

Cucumber Salad with Strawberry

Ingredients:

1 small cucumber

2 lettuce leaves

1 tbsp balsamic vinegar

2 tsp olive oil

¼ tsp white/black pepper

½ tsp ground oregano

1 tsp minced onion

½ cup strawberries, sliced

How to make:

Wash cucumber and slice it about ¼ inches thick. Mix all the ingredients except the lettuce. Spread lettuce leaves in a lunch box and add the mix cucumber salad. Add strawberries on the side.

Broccoli with Seasoned Herb

Ingredients:

1-cup fresh broccoli

1 tsp chicken seasoning

½-cup hot water

1 tbsp butter

¼ tsp onion powder nutmeg

¼ tsp basil leaves

How to make:

Combine water and seasoned stock base, pour it over broccoli in a saucepan, and sprinkle it with seasoning. Let it boil then separate the broccoli and drain it. Add butter and serve with cream lemon-butter sauce.

Carrots with Parsley Cream

Ingredients:

½ cup water

1 carrot thinly sliced

¼ cup chicken stock

1/4 cup yellow and white corn kernels

¼ cup green peas

1 carrot, sliced

½ tsp rosemary leaves

1 tbsp butter

½ tsp arrowroot

½ tsp parsley flakes

½ cup milk

1 tbsp chopped onions

Dash of black pepper

How to make:

Combine green peas, corn kernels, celery, and crushed rosemary in a saucepan. Add the chicken stock and water. Pour it over the vegetables. Boil and let it simmer for 10 min.

Drain the vegetable and set aside. Melt butter and add the arrowroot, pepper, salt, milk, and onion. Cook over medium heat until the sauce thickens. Add parsley flakes and pour over the vegetables. Arrange in a lunchbox.

Squash in Apple Cider Vinegar

Ingredients:

1 cup cooked squash, shredded

½ tsp salt

1 tbsp butter

2 tbsp apple cider vinegar

Dash black pepper

¼ tsp cinnamon

¼ tsp mace

2 tbsp raisins

2 tbsp minced cherries

½-cup arugula leaves

How to make:

In a casserole dish, put the squash then add the pepper, cinnamon, mace, salt, and butter. Pour the apple cider vinegar over the squash and bake in the 350F oven for around 45 min.

Stir it once during the baking period. Let it cool. In a lunchbox, combine cooked squash, arugula, cherries, and raisins. Mix well.

Sautéed Asparagus

Ingredients:

1-cup fresh asparagus

1 tbsp butter

½ tsp soy sauce

Dash salt and pepper

½ tsp ginger

2 tbsp pecans

2 tbsp tomatoes, sliced

How to make:

Wash asparagus and slice it about ¼ inch thick. Melt butter and add salt, ginger, pepper, and mix it well. Add asparagus and toss gently. Cook over high heat for 2 min. Stir twice, add soy sauce and mix again. Serve in a lunch box with tomatoes and pecans.

Pepper Chili Bean

Ingredients:

40 gm black beans

20 gm corn kernels, drained

20 gm tomatoes, chopped

1 tbsp olive oil

1 small onion, chopped

40 gm red peppers, sliced

1 tsp chili powder

1 tsp ground cumin

1 tsp sweet smoked paprika

How to make:

Heat the oil. Sauté onion and add pepper, cook for 8 min. Put in the spices and cook for about a minute. Add in the tomatoes, beans, corn kernels, and simmer it for 15 min until chili is thick. Let it cool and serve in a lunchbox.

Eggplant Creole

Ingredients:

¼ cup cheese

1 eggplant

Dash of Salt and pepper

Flour

1 small garlic clove, minced

1 small onion, chopped

1 tbsp olive oil

¼-cup tomato soup

¼-cup water

How to make:

Wash eggplant and slice. Sprinkle pepper, salt to taste, and dredge it in flour. Fry it slowly and drain afterward. Sauté onion and garlic and add the tomato soup & water. Season it with salt and pepper to taste.

Arrange fried eggplant in a serving dish, pour tomato mixture, and top it with cheese. Bake it for 20 min and let it cool. Heat in the microwave when ready to eat at work.

Pasta

Recipes

Pasta with Tuna, Capers, and Olives

Ingredients:

70 gm dried pasta

40 gm canned tuna chunks, drained

1 tbsp chopped flat-leaf parsley

1 tbsp olive oil

2 tbsp butter

1 small garlic clove, sliced

1 tbsp lemon juice

2 tsp capers, drained

¼ cup black olives, sliced

Dash of Salt

How to make:

Cook the pasta according to the packet instructions.

Drain and return to the pan.

Heat the oil over medium-low heat and melt butter in

it. Add the garlic, tuna, lemon juice, capers, and olives.

Stir all the ingredients gently until completely heated.

Transfer the pasta to a serving dish. Toss the tuna mixture over the pasta and add the parsley and remaining butter.

Pasta with Rotisserie Chicken

What you need:

70 gm dried fettuccine pasta

40 gm leftover rotisserie chicken, chopped

20 gm leftover roasted vegetables

2 tbsp sun-dried-tomato pesto

Dash of Ground black pepper

2 tbsp Parmesan cheese

¼ cup mixed green peas

Balsamic vinegar

Dash of Salt

How to make:

Cook pasta according to packet instructions. Drain it and transfer half of it to a storage container. Drizzle it lightly with oil and toss to coat. Let it cool and then refrigerate.

Return the remaining fettuccine to the cooking pot then add chicken, vegetables, and pesto. Toss to coat the pasta and season it to taste with salt and pepper. Grate some parmesan cheese and sprinkle it on top. Prepare the mixed-green peas salad drizzled with the balsamic vinegar.

Olive Pesto Pasta

Ingredients:

70 gm dried penne

40 grams olives

2 tbsp fresh pesto

1 tbsp olive oil

1 garlic clove, chopped

1 tsp crushed chili flakes

1 tbsp ricotta

Parmesan, for garnish (optional)

How to make:

Heat the oil and add garlic, cook for 2 minutes until golden. Add the chili flakes and olives. Season it well. Let it simmer for 15 minutes until the sauce is thick.

Cook the penne according to the packet instructions. Drain and stir into the sauce. Top with a tbsp of ricotta and pesto plus shavings of parmesan cheese.

Chicken Penne Pasta

Ingredients:

70 gm dried penne

40 gm boneless chicken breasts cut into strips

1 tbsp olive oil

1 tbsp spring onions, chopped

20 gm feta cheese, diced

1 tbsp fresh chives

Dash Salt and pepper

How to make:

Heat the oil, add the chicken, and cook over medium heat for 5-8 minutes, or until golden. Add spring onions and cook for another 2 minutes. Stir feta cheese into the frying pan together with half the chives, put a dash of salt, and pepper to taste.

Boil lightly salted water and add the pasta, then let it boil for another 8-10 minutes.

Drain well and spoon the chicken mixture onto the pasta, toss lightly and serve immediately.

Broccoli and Chicken Pasta

Ingredients:

40 gm skinless, boneless chicken breasts, diced

10 gm roasted red peppers, diced

10 gm small broccoli florets

1 tbsp olive oil

2 tbsp melted butter

1 garlic clove, chopped

¼ tsp dried chili flakes

70 gm dried Farfalle

½-cup chicken stock

Salt and pepper

How to make:

Boil the salted water. In another pan, heat the oil and butter over medium-low heat. Add the garlic then slowly add the chicken, increase to heat and cook for 5 min. Sprinkle chili flakes and season with salt and pepper to taste. Set aside.

Bring the broccoli into the boiling water and cook for 2 minutes then set aside.

Cook pasta for 8-10 minutes, or until tender but still firm to the bite. Drain and add the pasta to the chicken mixture in a separate frying pan. Add roasted peppers and broccoli and pour in the stock. Simmer it again, over medium-high heat, stirring frequently.

Chicken & Basil Fettuccine Pasta

Ingredients:

40 gm boneless chicken breasts

70 gm dried fettuccine

Spring or fresh basil, to garnish

Dash of Salt and pepper

1 tbsp olive oil

Pesto:

1 tbsp freshly grated pecorino cheese

10 gm grated parmesan cheese

20 gm shredded fresh basil

4 tbsp ml extra virgin olive oil

1 tbsp pine kernels

1 garlic cloves, crushed

Dash of Salt

How to make:

Prepare the pesto first by combining the olive oil, pine kernels, basil, garlic and a pinch of salt and blend it using blender or food processor. Process the ingredients until smooth, transfer the mixture to a bowl, and stir in the cheese.

Heat the oil on a medium flame and cook the chicken breasts for 8-10 minutes. Cut it into small cubes.

Meanwhile, bring to boil lightly salted water. Add the pasta, and boil it for another 8-10 minutes. Drain and transfer the pasta to lunch box and add the chicken and pesto.

Tuna Pasta with Parsley

Ingredients:

70 gm dried pasta

40 gm canned tuna chunks, drained

1 tbsp chopped flat-leaf parsley

2 tsp olive oil

2 tsp melted butter

1 small garlic clove, sliced

1 tbsp lemon juice

2 tbsp green beans, drained

2 tbsp black olives, sliced

Dash of Salt

How to make:

Cook the pasta according to the packet instructions.

Drain and return to the pan.

Heat the oil over a medium-low heat and melt butter in it. Add the garlic, tuna, lemon juice, green beans, and olives. Stir all the ingredients gently until completely heated.

Transfer the pasta to a lunch box. Toss the tuna mixture over the pasta and add the parsley and remaining butter.

Quick Tuna Spaghetti

Ingredients:

70 gm dried spaghetti

40 gm canned tuna, drained

50ml chicken stock

1 tbsp olive oil

1 tomato peeled, chopped

20 gm mushrooms, sliced

2 tsp shredded fresh basil

1 small garlic clove, chopped

½ tsp dried marjoram

Dash of Salt and pepper

50 gm grated parmesan cheese

How to make:

Heat the oil in a frying pan. Add the tomatoes and cook over a low heat for 15 min.

Add the mushrooms and stir occasionally, for another 10 minutes. Add in the tuna, basil, stock, garlic and marjoram and season with a dash of salt and pepper to give taste. Cook over a low heat for 5 about minutes

Boil lightly salted water and add pasta, then boil again for another 10 min.

Drain the pasta, transfer to a lunch box, and pour over the tuna mixture. Add grated parmesan cheese if you wish.

Smoked Salmon & Arugula Pasta

Ingredients:

50 gm smoked salmon

70 gm dried fusilli

2 tsp fresh dill, plus extra sprigs to garnish

50 grams arugula

1 tbsp unsalted butter

1 small onion, chopped

1 tbsp white wine

¼-cup double cream

2 tsp lemon juice

Dash of Salt and pepper

How to make:

Cook the pasta according to the packet instructions.

Melt the butter in a heavy-based saucepan. Add onion and cook over a low heat for 5 minutes.

Add the wine, let it boil and continue boiling until reduced by two thirds. Pour the cream, put salt, and pepper to taste. Bring to the boil again, reduce the heat, and simmer it again for another 2 minutes. Cut the smoked salmon into squares, put into the saucepan, and stir it with the snipped dill and lemon juice to taste.

Drain the pasta and transfer to a dish. Add the salmon mixture, toss well, and garnish it with dill sprigs and arugula. Serve in a lunch box.

Salmon in Soured Cream Pasta

Ingredients:

70 gm dried pasta

40 gm mushrooms

1 tsp Dijon mustard

¼ cup soured cream

¾ cup of diced tomatoes, broccoli florets, and diced

cucumber tomatoes

1 tbsp spring onions, minced

Grated rind of ½ lemon

Dash of Salt and pepper

How to make:

Boil water and add the pasta, bring back to the boil

and cook for 8-10 min. Drain the pasta and return to

the pan.

Add the mushrooms, mustard, soured cream, spring onions, broccoli, cucumber, and lemon rind to the pasta. Stir over a low heat and season to taste with pepper.

Transfer to a lunch box and sprinkle the chives over the top.

Seafood

Recipes

Codfish Lunchbox Dish

Ingredients:

110 gm codfish

2 tsp extra-virgin olive oil

Flour for dusting

1 clove of garlic, minced

2 tsp sherry vinegar

Small Lemon wedges

½ tsp chili flakes

2 tsp brown sugar

For the mash:

Finely chopped parsley

1 tsp melted butter

1 small head celeriac (peeled & cubed)

How to make:

The first step is to prepare the mash, boil the celeriac for about 10 min in salted water and drain it afterward. Mash with seasoning & butter and stir in the parsley. Keep it warm while you cook the fish.

Dust the fish with flour and fry it for about 4 minutes on each side. Put it aside once done. Cook the garlic and chili in a separate pan for about 2 min until golden brown. Add the sugar, vinegar, salt and bubble it for 2 min.

Serve the fish together with the mash. Pour over the sauce on top of the fish. Sprinkle the remaining parsley on top and arrange the lemon wedges on the side.

Baked Bluefish in Garlic & Lime Sauce

Ingredients:

110 gm bluefish fillet

1 tbsp virgin olive oil

¼ tsp red pepper flakes

Dash of Salt

1 clove garlic, minced

1 small lemon, cut into wedges

2 tsp lemon juice

50 grams spinach (steamed)

How to make:

Preheat baking dish in the oven to 220C (425F).

Combine the red pepper flakes & garlic with the oil in a small bowl. Rub the fish fillets with the garlic mixture & sprinkle salt to taste.

Put the fillets in the preheated baking dish with the skin side facing down together with the limes. Bake for 10-15 min. Serve with squeezed limes over the fish and steamed spinach.

Salmon with Lemons, Onions & Herbs

Ingredients:

¼ lb. Salmon fillet

2 tsp apple cider vinegar

¼ tsp salt

1 small onion, chopped

1 small lemon, cut into wedges

1 tbsp mixed herbs (parsley, oregano, cilantro, mint)

1 tsp olive oil

How to make:

Put the salmon in a roasting pan and pour water enough to cover the salmon. Add the vinegar and salt and bring the water to a boil over high heat. Turn off the flame and let the salmon stand for about 30 min.

In a blender, mix herbs and ¼ cup olive oil. Blend until smooth.

Transfer the salmon to a lunch box using a spatula. Add lemon wedges and season with mixed herbs.

Prawn with Basil & Thyme

Ingredients:

¼ lb. prawns (peeled)

1 tbsp butter

½ piece of green bell pepper, diced

1 celery rib, chopped

1 small white onion, chopped

1 clove garlic, chopped

¼ can diced tomatoes

3 tbsp double cream

¼ can small button mushroom, sliced and drained

1 tbsp fresh basil, chopped

1 tsp fresh thyme, chopped

Dash of salt and pepper

½ piece jalapeno, chopped

2 tsp lemon juice

How to make:

Melt the butter over medium-high heat. Sauté garlic for about 30 seconds then add the bell pepper, onion & celery. Cook for about 4 min. Add mushroom & tomatoes, bring heat to medium, and simmer until sauce thickens.

Stir in cream, lemon juice, jalapeno & prawns. Reduce to medium-low heat, cover and let it simmer for about 4 minutes. Put salt & pepper to taste and stir in basil & thyme.

Prawns in Apple Cider Vinegar

Ingredients:

110 gm prawns (shell-on)

1 tbsp apple cider vinegar

1-cup water

½ tsp salt

2 tsp pickling spice

How to make:

Boil the water over high heat, and then add vinegar, pickling spice, and salt. Reduce heat to medium and simmer it for another 20 minutes.

Bring back the mixture to boil over high heat. Add prawns & turn off the heat, cover and let stand for about 4 minutes or until prawn turns pink. Serve in a lunchbox with cooked pasta and oranges.

Catfish with minced Almond

Ingredients:

110 gm catfish, sliced

1 egg

1 tbsp rapeseed oil

2 tsp cold water

2 tsp Cajun spice blend

¼ tsp salt

30 gm all-purpose baking mix

15 gm minced almond

1 tsp soy sauce

2 tsp lemon juice

1 small onion, minced

¼-cup vegetable stock

How to make:

Dredge the catfish in the baking mix together with minced almond. Add ¼-cup vegetable stock and cook in a saucepan.

Simmer for 10 minutes until cooked. Season with lemon juice, minced onion, and soy sauce. Serve with brown rice in a lunchbox.

Grilled Swordfish Steaks

Ingredients:

110 gm skinless swordfish

1 tbsp lemon juice

1 tbsp virgin olive oil

1 clove garlic, chopped

Dash of Salt

Dash of Ground black pepper

10 gm pitted black olives

2 tsp mixed herbs

1 small tomato, diced

How to make:

Marinate the swordfish in a mixture of combined oil, lemon juice & garlic in a serving dish. Transfer about 1 tbsp of the mixture in a separate bowl & set aside. Refrigerate it for about 20 minutes, turning steaks once.

Grill the fish and season with salt and pepper to taste.

Take the reserved marinade and add tomato, olives, and herbs. Toss gently and season it with salt and pepper. Serve the fish fillets with marinade sauce on top.

Prawns with Mushrooms

Ingredients:

¼ lb. prawns

¼ can mushrooms

1 tsp minced onion

1 tbsp butter

Dash of pepper

2 tsp mustard

1 tbsp lemon juice

1tsp Worcestershire sauce

1 tsp Sherry wine

1 tbsp flour

1 tbsp cream

How to make:

Sauté the onion in butter, add the remaining ingredients, and mix it thoroughly. Cook over low heat for 5 min.

Place prawns and cooked mixture in a baking dish. Add cream on top and bake it for 15 min in 450F or until top portion is delicately brown.

Broiled Clams with Bacon

Ingredients:

6-7 pcs small clams in a half shell

1 sliced bacon

¼ tsp rock salt

Small dash mace

Dash of dry mustard

1 tsp butter

¼ tsp onion powder

½ tsp lemon peel

½ tsp shredded green onions

How to make:

Melt butter in the pan and add the seasoning ingredients. Spread salt in a baking pan then arrange the clams. Put 1 tsp of butter mixture over the clam. Cut bacon into pieces and sprinkle it on top of the clams. Preheat broiler and broil the clams for around 5 min or until lightly brown.

Spicy Shrimp in Vinegar

Ingredients:

¼ lb. fresh shrimp

¾-cup water

1 tbsp vinegar

1 tbsp pickled spice

1 tsp red pepper

½ tsp salt

How to make:

Boil water for 10 min and add the spices: salt and vinegar, and then add the shrimp. Let it boil for another 7 min until the prawn is completely cooked. Remove and let it stand for 20 min before draining it. Arrange in a lunchbox and add broccoli, grapes, and apples on the side.

Meat

Recipes

Baked Crispy Chicken Nuggets

Ingredients:

110 gm skinless chicken breast fillets

1 tbsp mayonnaise

10 gm crushed Whole-wheat breadcrumbs

10 gm breadcrumbs

How to make:

Preheat oven to 220C. Coat the chicken with mayonnaise in a separate bowl and stir well. Mix both breadcrumbs in a bowl. Coat the chicken with mayonnaise with breadcrumbs mixture.

Spread the coated chicken on a baking sheet and bake for 10 minutes until tender. Serve with cooked pasta, cucumber, and raspberries in a lunchbox.

Minute Steak with Mushroom

Ingredients:

110 grams minute steaks

50 grams button mushroom, sliced

1 tbsp olive oil

1 tbsp butter

½ tsp salt, divided

1 small white onion, sliced

¼ tsp ground black pepper

50 ml beef broth

¼ tsp paprika

1 tbsp parsley, chopped

2 tsp lemon juice

How to make:

Season the steak with salt and pepper. Put combined butter and oil in a frying pan over high heat. Add the steaks and sear until cooked. Transfer to the plate once done and keep warm.

Heat the remaining butter and oil in a separate frying pan over high heat. Sauté the mushrooms and onion for about 8 min. Add broth, juices from the steaks, lemon juice, paprika, salt, and pepper.

Cook until sauce thickens for about 3 minutes. Pour sauce over steaks & sprinkle with parsley.

Sautéed Italian Sausage

Ingredients:

110grams Italian sausages

1 head of fennel, sliced thin

1 tbsp red wine vinegar

1 tbsp olive oil

1 clove garlic, chopped

1 small onion, sliced

¼ tsp oregano powder

¼ tsp ground black pepper

¼ tsp salt

How to make:

Heat the oil over a medium flame. Add sausages and cook until browned for about 7 minutes. Transfer it to a platter and cover with foil to keep warm.

Heat the remaining oil over a medium-high flame. Add onion, occasionally stirring about 3 minutes then add fennel and cook for another minute. Stir in oregano, garlic, vinegar, salt, and pepper. Cook until vegetables are tender for about 5 minutes. Serve with apple and pecans.

Meatballs with Spicy Ketchup Sauce

Ingredients:

110 grams beef meatballs

1 tbsp chili sauce

3 tbsp ketchup

1 tsp maple syrup

How to make:

In a saucepan, cook meatballs until golden. Place on a plate with paper towel to removes excess oil.

In a mixing bowl, add chili sauce, ketchup, and maple syrup. Stir well. Place meatballs in a lunchbox together with the sauce. Serve with celery on the side.

Teriyaki Beef in Lemon Sauce

Ingredients:

¼ lb. beef tenderloin

½ tsp onion salt

2 tbsp soy sauce

2 tbsp brown sugar

1 tbsp lemon juice

½ tsp ground ginger

¼ tsp garlic powder

How to make:

Cut the tenderloin into bite-size cubes. Combine all the remaining ingredients, pour it over the beef cubes, and let it stand in the refrigerator for about an hour. Thread cubes on the skewer, alternate it with pineapple and sliced red pepper, and grill for around 10-12 min. Serve in a lunchbox.

Chicken Balls with Sweet Curry Sauce

Ingredients:

¼ lb. ground chicken

1 tsp salt

½ tsp onion powder

1 tbsp breadcrumbs

2 tsp curry powder

¼ cup flour

1 tsp maple syrup

¼ tsp pepper

3 tbsp melted butter

How to make:

Combine all ingredients in a mixing bowl except for butter and flour. Form bite-size balls and roll it with flour. Sauté for 15 min in the butter until golden brown. Serve it in a lunchbox with the sweet curry sauce.

Roasted Lamb with Herbs

Ingredients:

4 oz. rib-rack of lamb

¼ tsp thyme

¼ tsp black pepper

½ tsp salt

⅛ tsp onion powder

1 cup quinoa, cooked

¼ cup steamed squash, diced

A dash of Parsley leaves

How to make:

Combine all the ingredients and rub it in the lamb.
Place it on a rack and bake it in a 325F oven for around
30 min. Slice the lamb into strips and mix it with
cooked quinoa. Add steamed squash and sprinkle with
parsley. Transfer it to a lunchbox.

Roasted Chicken with Vegetables

Ingredients:

4 oz. cooked chicken, diced

2 ½ tsp olive oil

1 tbsp balsamic vinegar

1 tsp maple syrup

¼ cup tomatoes, sliced

½ cup chopped lettuce

A few pieces of Raspberries and blueberries

How to make:

Roast the chicken until golden and then set aside. In a mixing bowl, combine olive oil, vinegar, maple syrup, tomatoes and chopped lettuce. Stir well and then add the roasted chicken. Serve in a lunchbox with raspberries and blueberries.

Chicken with Herbs

Ingredients:

¼ lb. chicken

2 tsp minced onion

¼ cup flour

1 tsp parsley

1 tbsp season-all powder

½ tsp thyme leaves

¼ tsp black pepper

½ cup dry white wine

½ tsp paprika

½ tsp herb seasoning

2 tbsp butter

How to make:

Cut chicken into pieces. Meanwhile, combine flour, pepper, paprika, & herb seasoning in a mixing bowl, mix well and dredge the chicken in it.

Grill until brown. Sprinkle parsley, onion, and thyme over the chicken. Serve with rice and steamed broccoli.

Ground Beef with Mushroom

Ingredients:

¼ lb. ground beef

½ tsp mustard

1 egg beaten

¼-cup breadcrumbs

¼-cup celery

½ tsp minced onion

¼ can mushroom

1 tsp powdered horseradish

¼-cup mushroom liquid

1 tsp salt

Hot to make:

Mix all ingredients in a mixing bowl. Cook in a saucepan over medium heat. Stir frequently while cooking. When the meat turns golden brown, transfer to a lunchbox and season with parsley.

Conclusion

Good diet and nutrition start with the food that we eat. Most of us do not bother to know the importance of having a well-balanced diet in life. The recipes provided in this cookbook will serve as a guide for planning a healthy meal for your family especially for those people who are always on the go.

Meal planning saves a lot of your energy, money and of course your precious time as it provides a strategic way of being organized and efficient in your kitchen. We need to realize that expensive food does not necessarily be the most nutritious one and neither the cheaper food might be lacking enough nutrients.

Wise substitution in food or ingredients will give you enough money to save and use for other needs.

Finally, if you enjoyed this book, please take the time to share your thoughts and post a review on Amazon. It would be greatly appreciated!

Made in the USA
Middletown, DE
08 April 2018